FASHION
OF THE
SOUL

A book of aphorisms

SECOND EDITION

FASHION
OF THE
SOUL

A book of aphorisms
by
AMIR YASHAR AJAMI

First published by Yashar Publishing, in 2006
www.yashaar.com

ISBN-10: 1-4196-9010-8
ISBN-13: 978-1-4196-9010-5

Cover Designed by Nahal Sohbati
Book Designed by Ehsan Farid Afshar

Printed and bound in the United States
by
BookSurge Publishing
www.booksurge.com
1-866-308-6235

SECOND EDITION

For my beloved Parents,
Davoud and Fazilat

Acknowledgments

My main source of inspiration has always been my parents' love for each other. I thank them for being who they are and allowing me to witness a rare example of true love. Among those who freely shared their time and expertise in implementing this book, I wish to offer my gratitude and acknowledgement first to Mahin Bahrami. Her meticulous translation of some of my works as well as her constant encouragement to write in English has increased my confidence in expressing myself in this language. Furthermore, I am indebted to Mr. J. Lobo for his selfless contributions and easy accessibility. His assistance in editing this book together with his insightful guidance and understanding has allowed this humble work to reach completion. I also wish to thank Ehsan Farid Afshar for his powerful images which have not only brought visual appeal to the text but have also lent a dimension of completeness to my writing. Finally, I must thank a dear family member and my close confidant, Ferial Soufi for her immense support throughout my creative years. Her steadfast support has been a pillar of strength during the most crucial times and I am forever indebted to her.

Introduction

The roots of Aphorism lie deep in Ancient Greece where the word *Aphorism*, meaning "to define", was first invented. Aphorism is essentially a compact phrase containing a known truth and the first collection of such phrases was found in the book of Aphorisms by the famous Greek physician Hippocrates in the 5th century B.C. By applying aphorisms to the art of healing Hippocrates defined symptoms and diagnosis of certain illnesses in a very compact yet comprehensible form. Probably his best known aphorism is, "Life is short, [the] art long, opportunity fleeting, experiment treacherous, judgment difficult." Over the centuries this distinct and versatile form of expression found its way into literature, poetry and religious books. Aphorism, also known as *wisdom literature,* was used by sages throughout the world to provide moral guidance for their followers. Many authors and philosophers through the centuries have used aphorisms to relay their complex thoughts and ideas in a condensed yet effective way. It is this aspect of efficiency that has some sociolinguists considering aphorism as a form of poetry.

And it is the love for poetry that compelled the author, Amir Yashar Ajami, to create this collection of aphorisms. His earlier poetic background rendered this choice of form as a natural progression in his literary development. Engulfed in a sea of entrepreneurship and consumerism, at the young age of sixteen, Ajami felt a deep sense of alienation and began his solitary journey into the world of contemplation. He pondered over love, God, life, religion and existence. He questioned each concept and their socially accepted definitions. The prevalent hypocrisies and contradictions in the society around him served as catalysts to explore the world of poetry searching for harmony and beauty. Soon his thoughts became written words and after several years of pondering and meditation in search of inner peace he created his first collection of poetry written in his mother tongue, Persian. It was in the year 2004 when he was honoured by the Iranian Mystics Association with its fellowship and received the prestigious award recognizing him as one of the top seven Mystic Poets of Iran. The current collection of aphorisms, written in English, is a continuation of Ajami's exploration into human relationships and moral values. His unique perspective on life and everyday routine and an exceptional taste in aesthetics has allowed him to create highly thought provoking, yet elegant aphorisms that compel the reader to ponder over their inspirational truth while basking in their flowing rhythm. This collection is a result of years of reflection by the author and his meticulous choice of words. In addition, through a scrupulous process, a unique illustration is provided for each aphorism, complimenting and accentuating its essence. In this volume an innovative method of presentation is utilized whereby different art forms are combined to create an aesthetically balanced new art called, *Aphography*. It is the author's wish that through this medium the reader will find new perspectives on old issues that have engaged us all through the ages. This aim is in coherence with the author's belief that "Aphography is not just a static thought but a genuine motive for thinking".

MAHIN BAHRAMI

To love is not to create
a lover and a beloved.

To love is to transform
the lover into the beloved,
and the beloved into the lover
endlessly.

Love is not sedentary
but ever flowing.

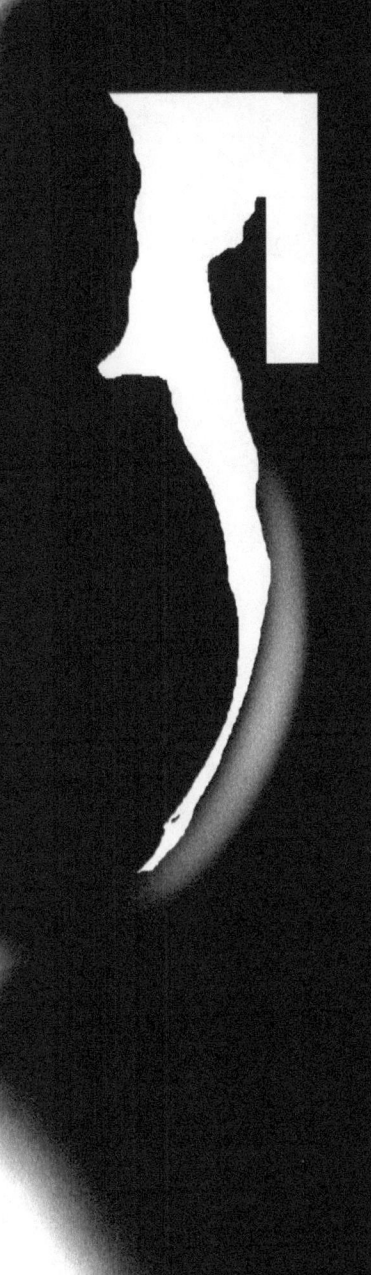

TO be in
love
with someone
or
something
is not
heretical.
Not being
in love
         is.

One who loves you for something, loves the thing.

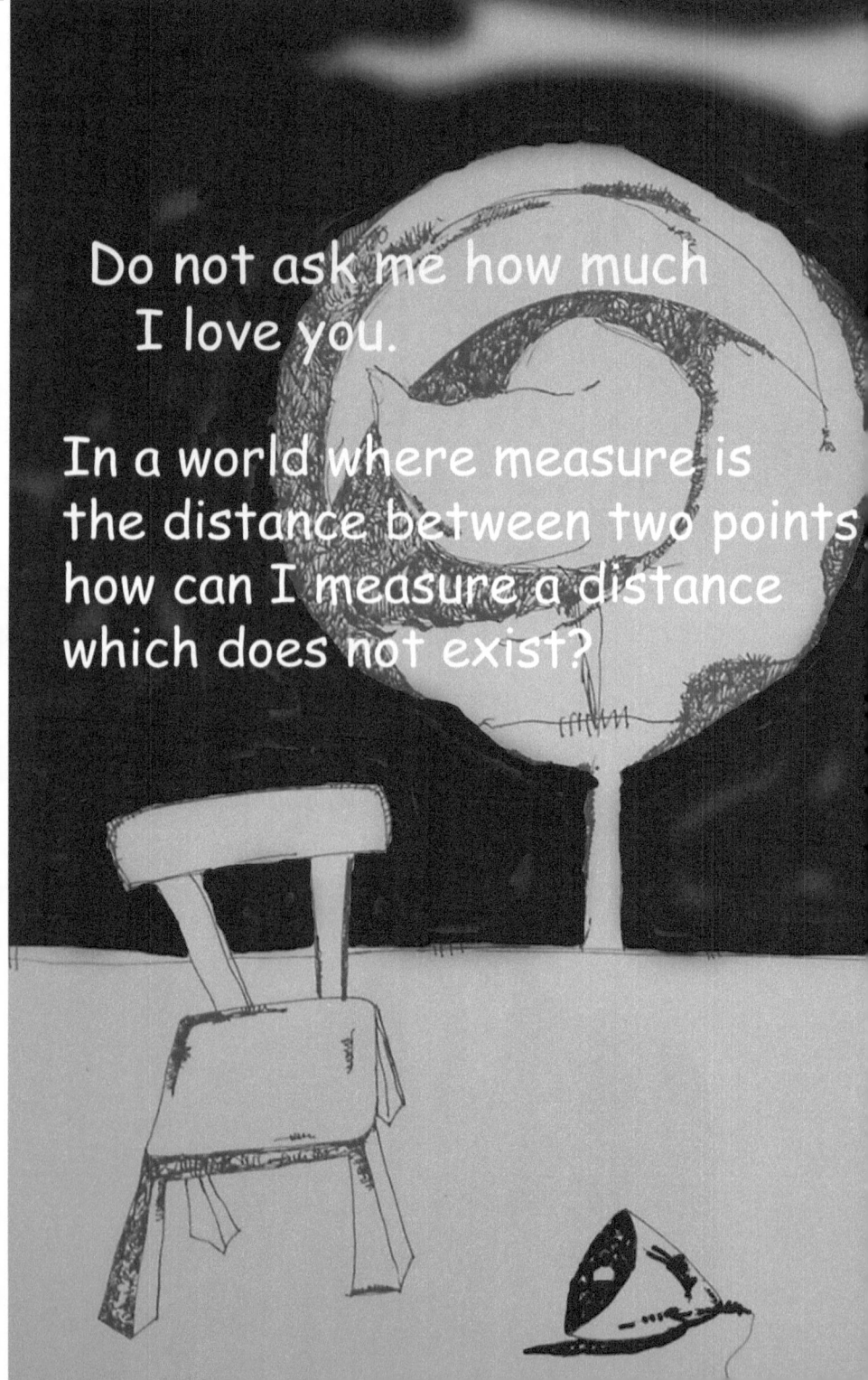

Do not ask me how much
   I love you.

In a world where measure is
the distance between two points
how can I measure a distance
which does not exist?

There is no "more"
in love.
If you want more
then
you are
not
in love.

The same truthfulness which can be observed in a lover's eyes can be felt in his touch. That is why

when the eyes are blinded the hands take over.

A Man sees with his eyes,
A lover speaks with his.

Dreams can

come true,

and the truth exceeds reality.

Hope is the creator of even that which does not wish to be.

Art is the artist's will
bequeath to society.

That is why artists become famous
posthumously.

Art is a piece of the artist,

and artists are lovers who have torn themselves

into
pieces.

These days,
'master pieces'
are kept in museums.

The Past is the last present, the future the next one.

A part of you is always dead; that is called the past.

When I was a child they used to say
a poet is one who creates poems.
When I became a poet, I realized that
it is the poem that creates the poet.

In my childhood, I never understood

the reason for censoring the names of certain body parts. Later, I realized that I should never utter beautiful things.

More than being afraid of death, we should be afraid of life itself.

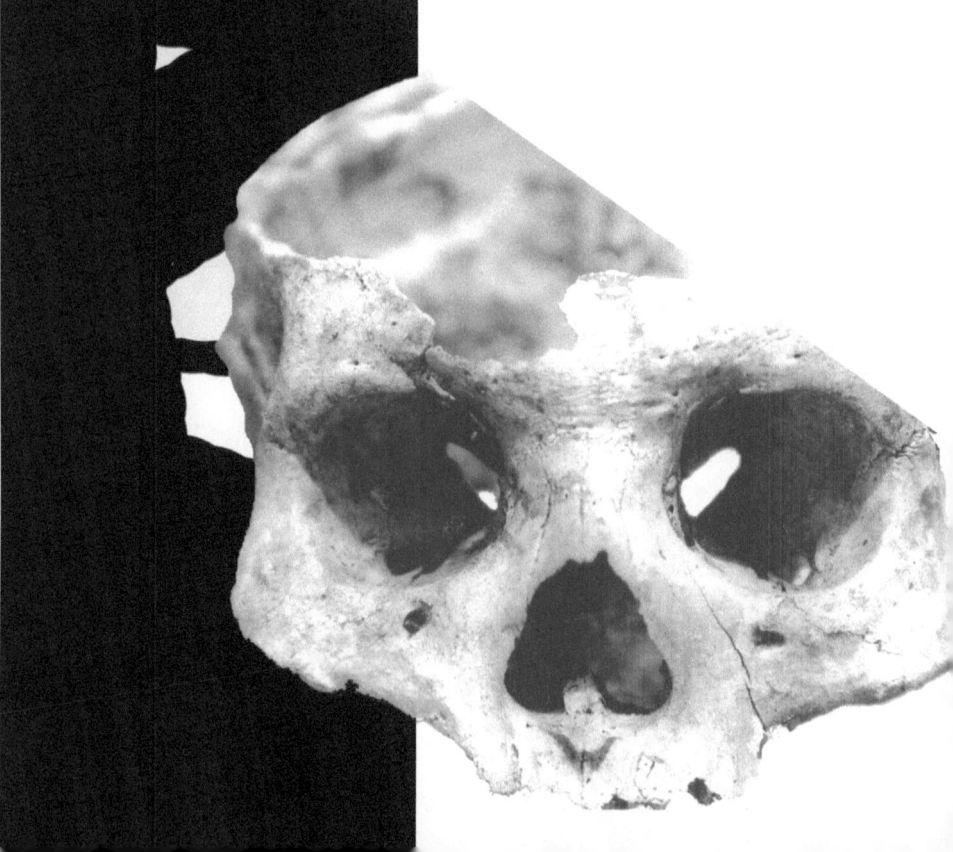

DEATH is not
 a disappearing;it
is the art of dissolving into
existence.

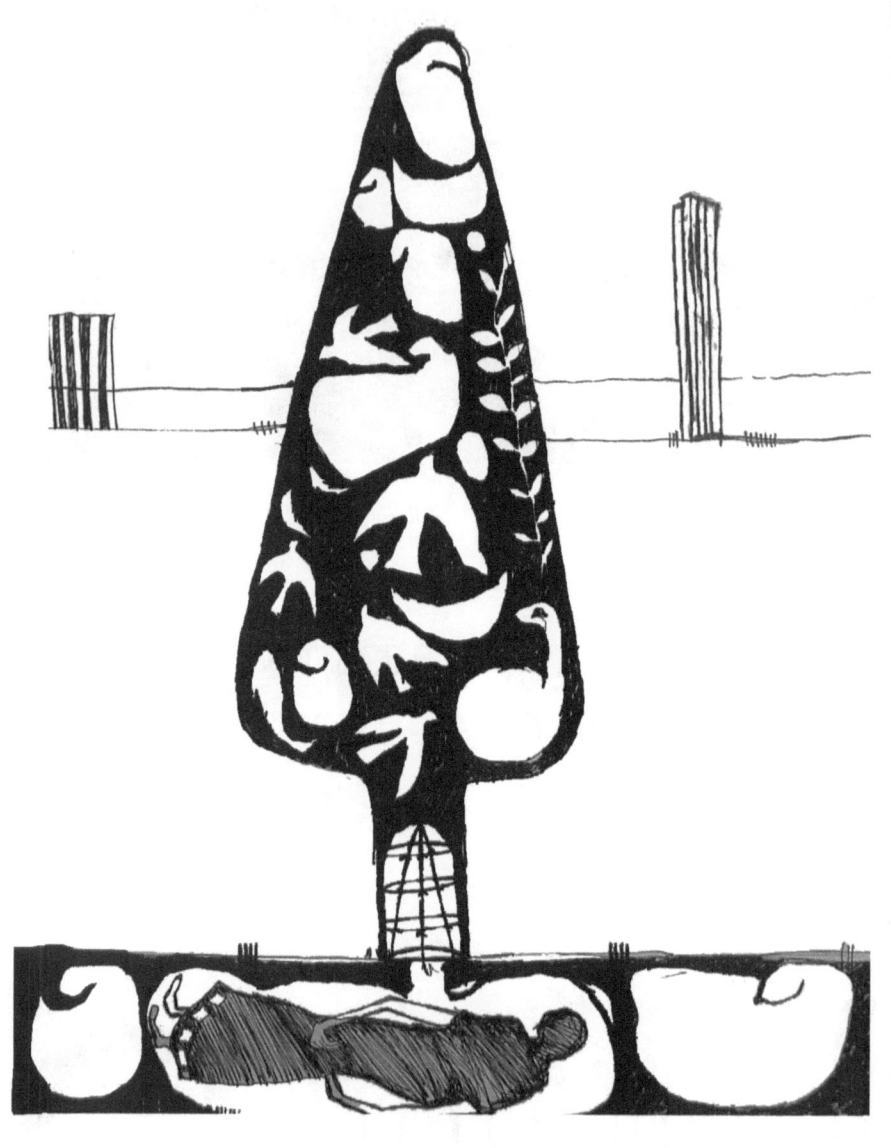

Death
is not an incident. It is a process.

"Nothing" - can

be understood,

but not

loved.

A fanatic person
is never truly pious.
Fanaticism
is a sign of faithlessness,
for faith is so great that it does
                  not require protection.

He is not brave who knows no fear;
in fact it is he who knows fear well
but fearlessness better.

Imagination is
reality traveling from
the future, to be recognized

a little earlier in the present.

I create poetry outside of time and space, for poetry is the tendency of Reality towards the Truth.

GRAVITY ALWAYS EXISTS,
AND ITS DIRECTION IS TOWARDS GREATNESS.
IT IS THE MAGNET WHICH IS ATTRACTED TO
THE LARGER STEEL.

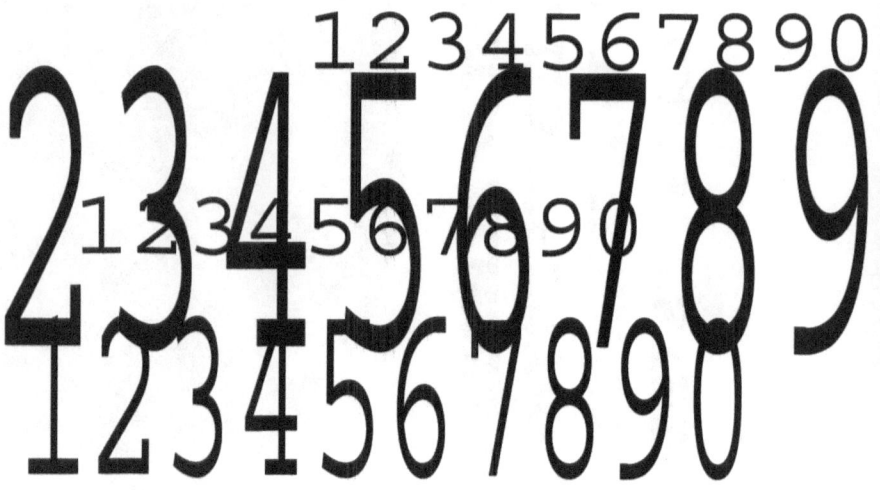

He who has created "One"
would never create Two.
But he who created Two,
created the crowd.

1

Once someone uttered "One", then others repeated One so often that all numbers came into existence. Yet no one has said more than One, and never will.

If Hell is the creation of God, then it must be a lovely place.

When all is beautiful then beauty is only a statement of preference.

Those who **love** windows are always **bound** by walls.

Paradoxically,
those who seek freedom
are always imprisoned. Perhaps

the pursuit of freedom is a trap

for true freedom fighters.

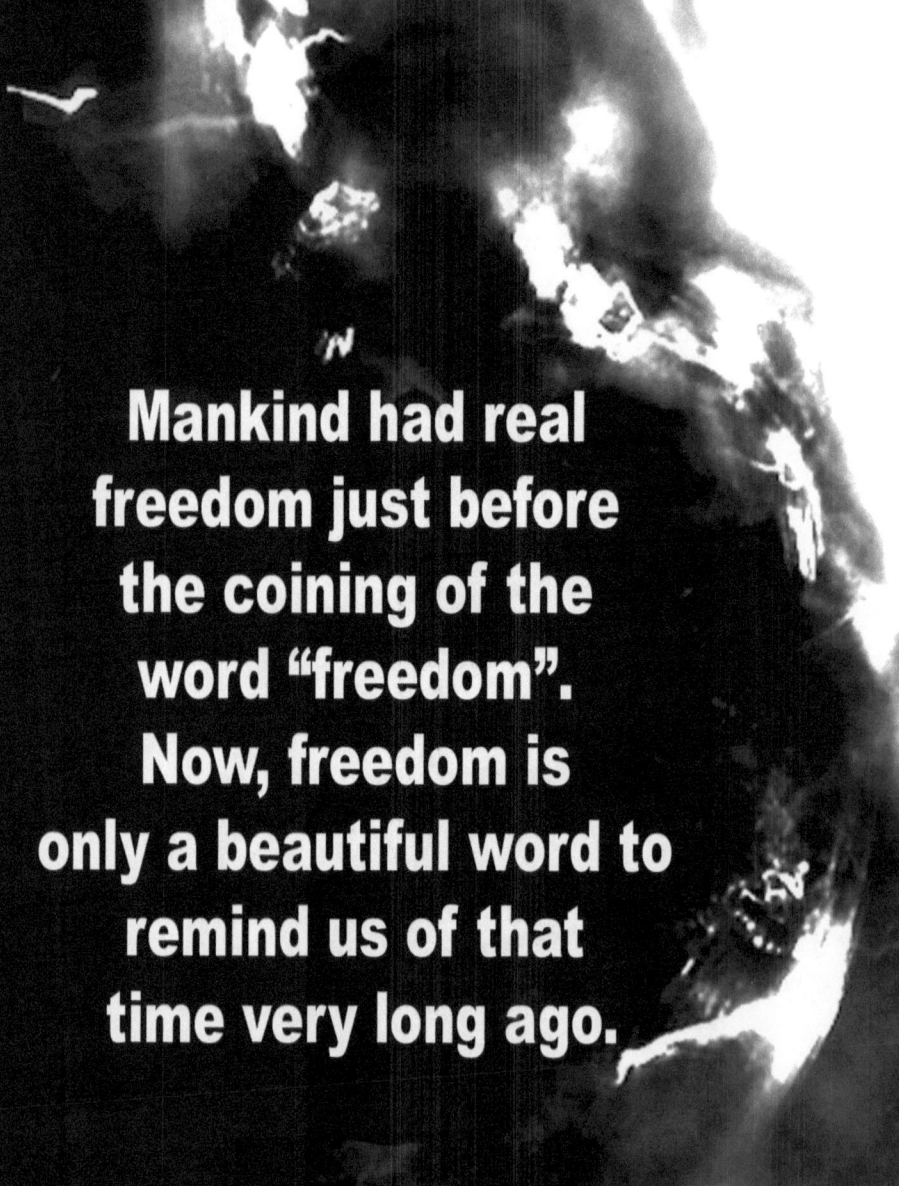

Mankind had real
freedom just before
the coining of the
word "freedom".
Now, freedom is
only a beautiful word to
remind us of that
time very long ago.

God forced us to be free,

so why

are we still
looking for
freedom?

ONLY THOSE WHO ARE AWAY FROM GOD SEEK AFTER HIM.

Why search for God?

Is he lost?

TO DEFEAT OPPRESSION,

iT iS FUTiLE TO REMOVE THE OPPRESSOR. THE CULTURE OF TOLERATING OPPRESSION SHOULD BE DESTROYED.

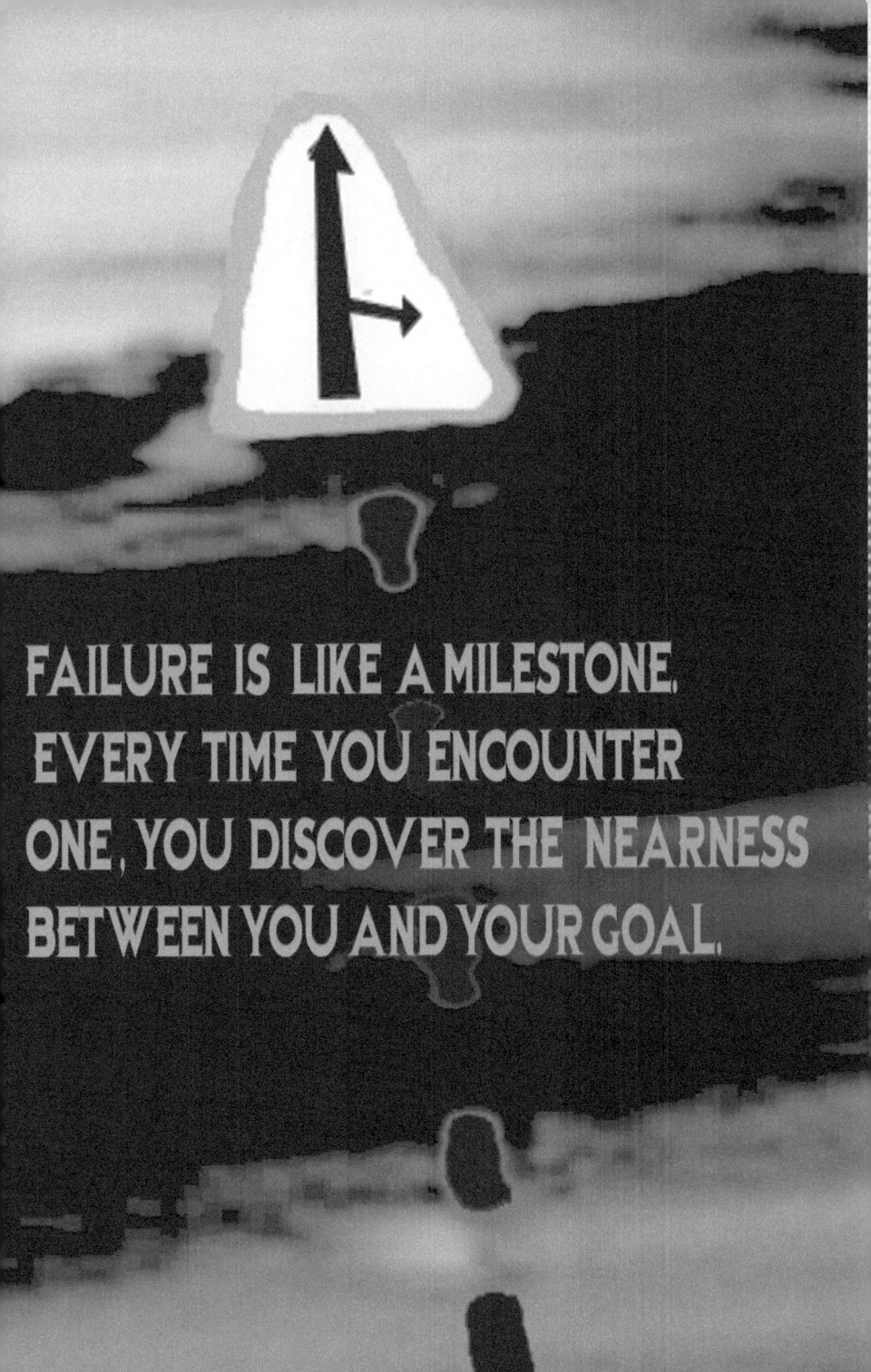

FAILURE IS LIKE A MILESTONE. EVERY TIME YOU ENCOUNTER ONE, YOU DISCOVER THE NEARNESS BETWEEN YOU AND YOUR GOAL.

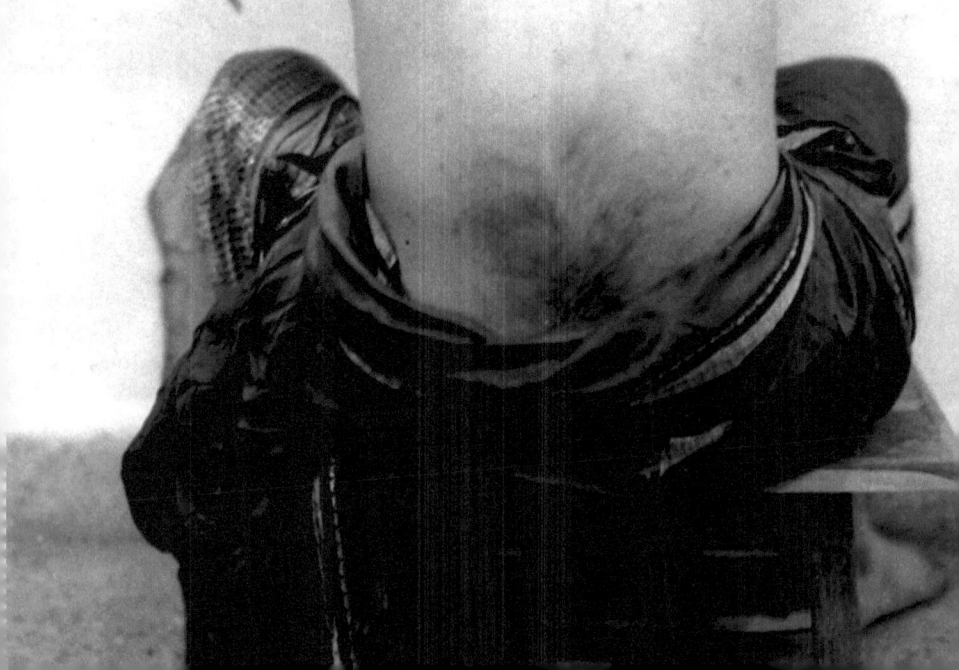

AND THE GOD WHO
MAY BE KNOWN, MAY
ALSO BE UNKNOWN.

BUT THE GOD WHO
MAY NOT BE KNOWN,
CANNOT BE UNKNOWN.

alone means only.

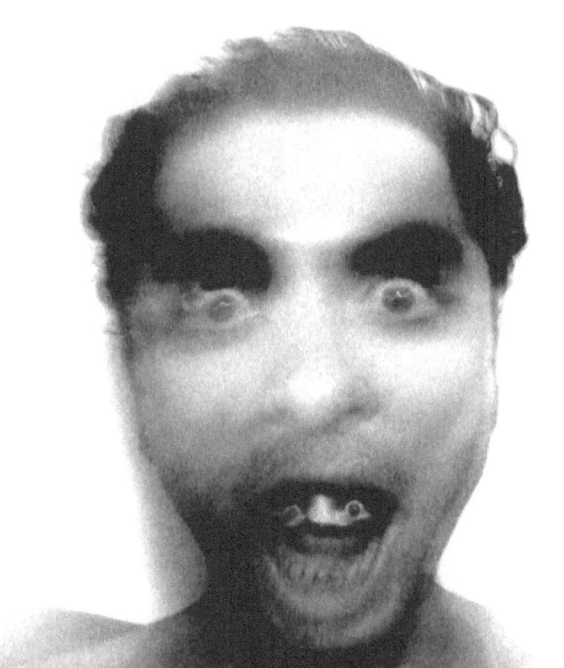

If Man had been born in Heaven, he would have searched for God on Earth.

GOD NEITHER EXISTS NOR DOES NOT. BUT HE MUST BE.

All that we know about God is his wisdom, not Himself.

When you deny God nothing will change. You will be the same and He will be the same. When you believe in Him you will be changed and He will still be the same.

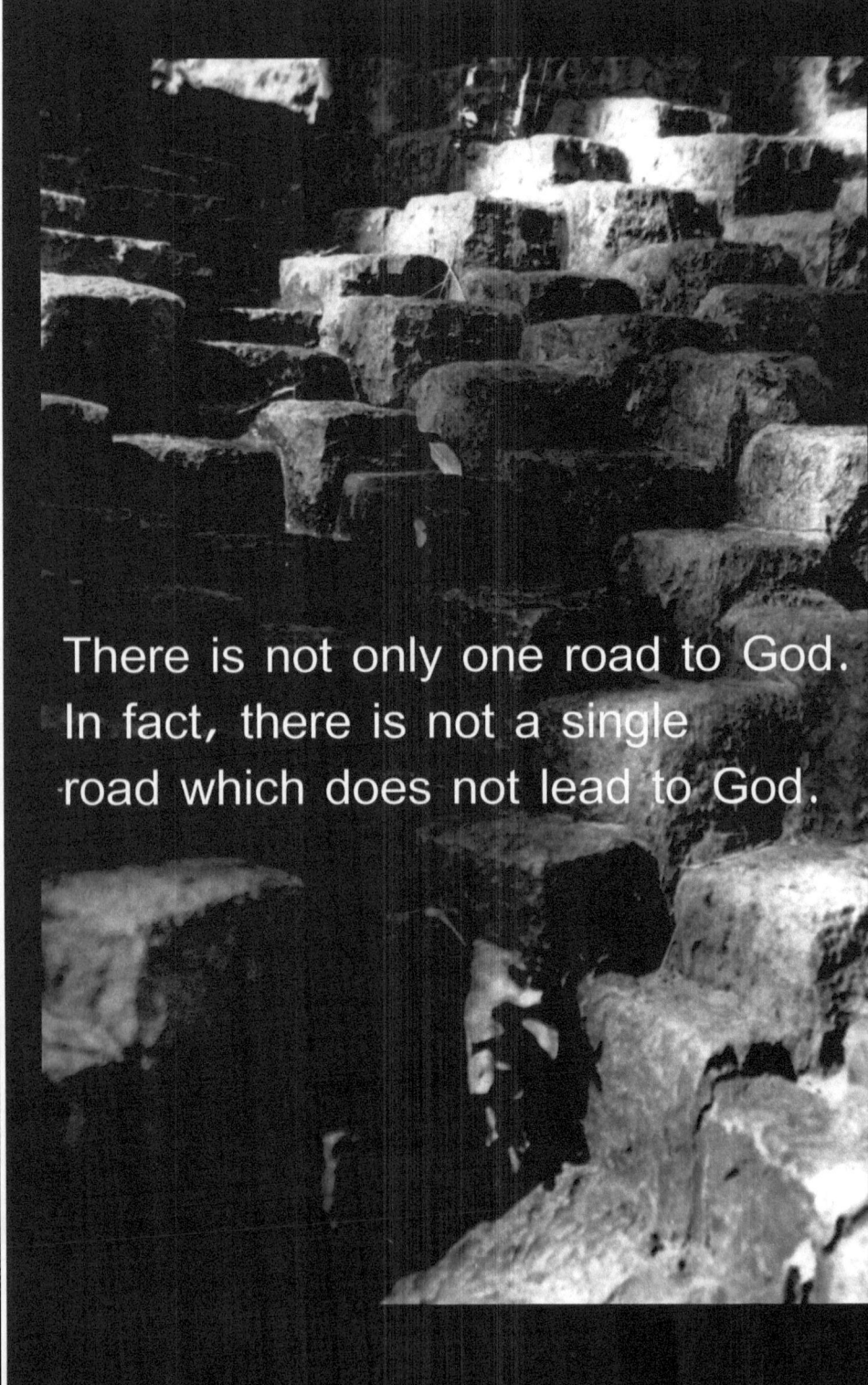

There is not only one road to God.
In fact, there is not a single
road which does not lead to God.

All that exists is a branch
of that single one,
which truly exists.

When you speak a foul word to your parents, recall the days they were eager to hear you talk.
Remember, the very first words which you learnt were their names.

TO UNDERSTAND THE TRUE
MEANING OF MOTHERHOOD,
YOUR UMBILICAL CORD
MUST STILL BE ATTACHED.

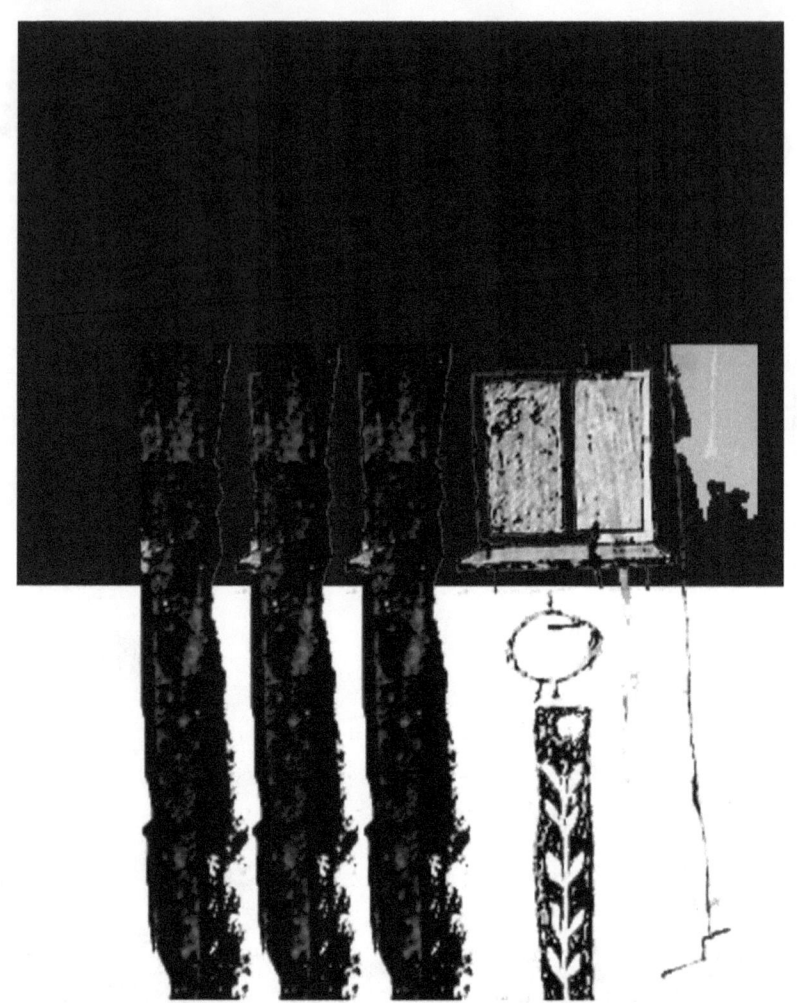

I am not alone

**for always "aloneness" is with me.
The one who takes away
my aloneness creates
my loneliness.**

The nature of sensible words is such that out of respect for hearing them all become silent. The nature of the most sensible words is such that out of respect for uttering them, one becomes silent.

The beauty of a smile is its purity; that's why tickling is never welcome.

The
true face of mankind is
a smiling one.

That
is the reason
we smile when
photographed.

A liar's sin is his fear, not his lie.

A liar is more one who refuses to reveal his lie than one who lies.

Whenever someone breaks your heart, do not be angry with him, for you have mistaken him for someone else.

There is no past, no future.
Both come to exist
in the present.

If "aloneness" drove me
towards you,
I desire that very aloneness,
and if "you"
drove me towards you,
I passionately desire you.
Leave me not alone.

If a jealous person knew that jealousy means "I am inferior", would he still be jealous?

What you wish
to hear from
my mouth,
see it in my
eyes and
taste it
on

my

lips.

You do not marry

when you are grown up.

You marry when you have grown up
sufficiently to know
you need someone
to grow up with.

When burning in love, I touch you, it is enough to make you fall in love a thousand times.
Touch is the 'heat conductor' of love.

When I am eager to hear a word from you, your silence becomes deafening.

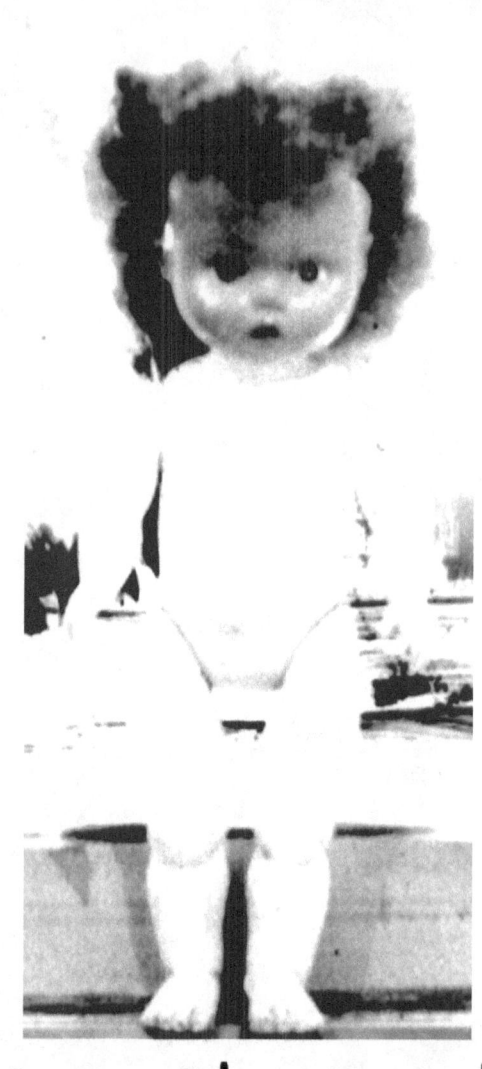

Sleeping with you is living
in paradise even when
I am asleep!

**Making love is two lovers
conversing without a word.**

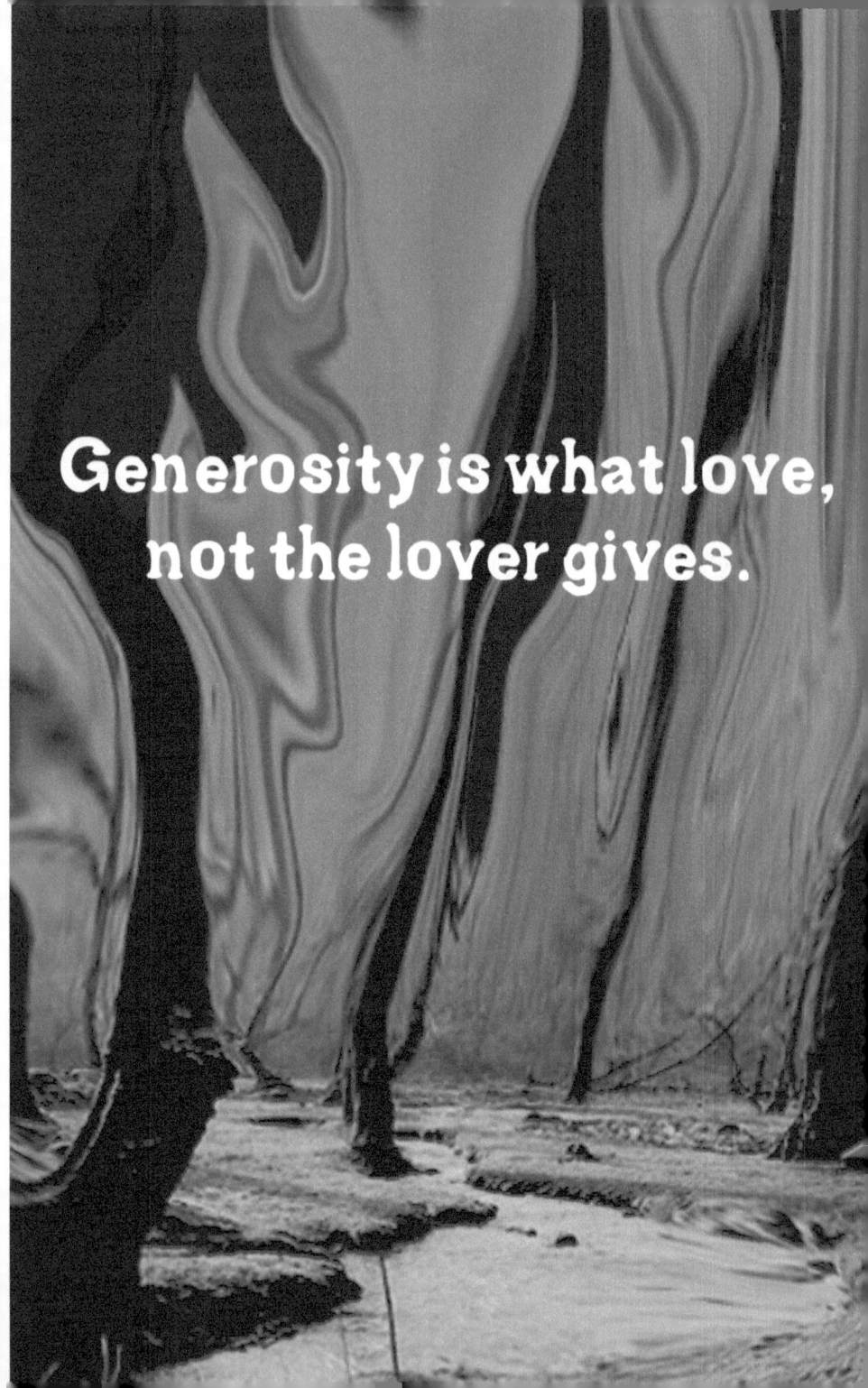

Generosity is what love,
not the lover gives.

Man's appreciation of
beauty destroys freedom.
The more beautiful, the greater the risk
of being captured.

wretchedness is forgetting
the happiness that surrounds you.

He, who mocks you,
does so to reduce one
of the many who may mock him.
He is afraid of himself.

'Hell is not being in love.'

"What is Good?"

is impossible to understand,

whether with one "O" or two.

We are forever.
And forever must be
realized in every possible
moment.

A birthday party is an excuse to honor your presence, your being, your existence. You are the celebration.

MAN ALWAYS ASSUMES THAT
IT IS HE WHO SEES LIGHT,
UNAWARE THAT BECAUSE
THERE IS THE LIGHT, THEREFORE
HE CAN SEE.

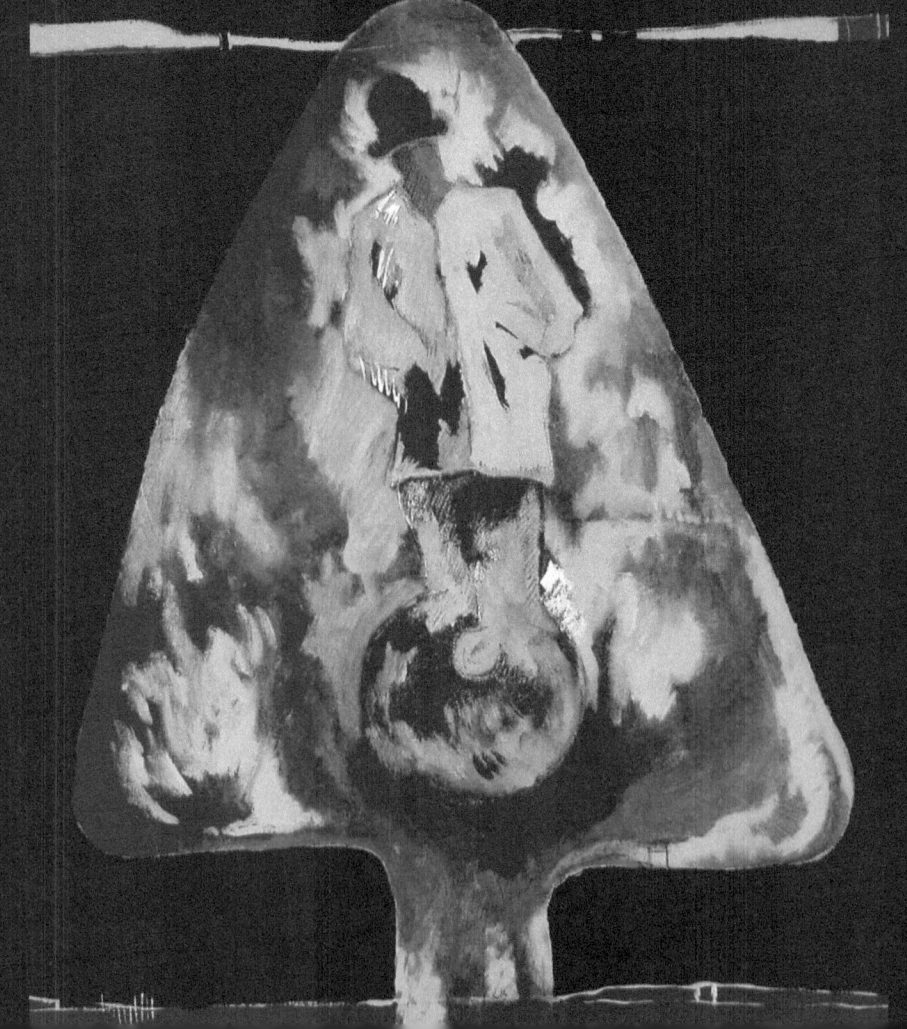

The apple
knew about gravity,
before
Newton.

Light does not need proof.
When you see, it is your
vision that is proven not
the Light.

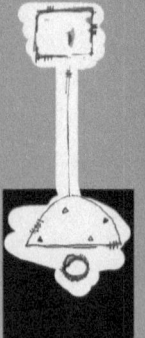

GOOD NEVER EXISTS WHEN THERE IS ALWAYS BETTER.

The best cannot exist either; it is just a reason to become better.

Once someone said that he
had no religion.
I gave him mine.

Now I have no
religion but
someone is
religious because
of me.

With love, even
bereft of
religion, one
becomes a
prophet.

THE HOLIEST BOOK
OF ALL

IS THE

UNWRITTEN ONE,

FOR GOD

TALKS WITH

SILENCE,

NOT WITH WORDS.

Democracy means
we decide for you that
you decide what we have decided.

A clever politician never deals with politics.

TRUTH IS SHY.

IT ALWAYS HIDES BEHIND WHAT IS IN PLAIN SIGHT.

Religion: fashion of the soul.

Civilization is the artificial wildness created by humans against the original one.

When the majority is always right how can genius be appreciated?!!!

MUSIC

Music is the art of presenting silence, what you enjoy is the silence between the sounds.

Luck is a strange gift. You never know when you paid for it or when you will.

123564768898998

I dance, for I am not matter.

THERE ARE DIFFERENT TYPES OF MEN BUT EVERY SINGLE WOMAN IS DIFFERENT FROM ANOTHER!

*When there is no conflict,
there comes no understanding,
but if there is understanding
there is no conflict.*

In Persia we say:
"everyone's destiny is written
on his forehead."

I cannot read my forehead but
I know there is only you there.

In the emptiness of my solitude,
you are my only answer.
I know nothing of you.
That is enough for me.

WHENEVER YOU LOAN SOMETHING, GIVE IT AWAY AS A GIFT. AND WHENEVER IT IS RETURNED, TAKE IT BACK AS A GIFT.

Fashion is the art of hiding beauty.

I have **cried** much
so that I
may
laugh honestly.

A mother's labor pain is proof of
a father's love. For, witnessing
your beloved's pain is more painful
than suffering from the pain yourself.

www.ingramcontent.com/pod-product-compliance
Lightning Source LLC
Chambersburg PA
CBHW030353290526
45785CB00004B/1723